Have fun
my **love**

Don't forget
to **smile** always

FUN & EASY
CURSIVE
(22 LETTERS ACTIVITIES)

BY
ALVIRA HARRIS

WE BELIEVE IT IS STILL SO IMPORTANT TO TEACH YOUR CHILDREN THE ART AND SKILL OF CURSIVE HANDWRITING. EVEN IN THIS DIGITAL AGE, PUTTING PEN TO PAPER IS KNOW TO STIMULATE THE BRAIN MORE THAN ANYTHING ELSE. HERE ARE JUST A FEW OF THE BENEFITS:

1. AS CHILDREN GROW INTO ADULTS THEY WILL NEED TO SIGN THEIR NAME ON ALL SORTS OF IMPORTANT DOCUMENTS. CURSIVE HELPS THEM DEVELOP A UNIQUE SIGNATURE. RESEARCH HAS SHOWN THAT CURSIVE SIGNATURES ARE HARDER TO FORGE THAN PRINT.

2. RESEARCH HAS SUGGESTED THAT WRITING CURSIVE LETTERS ACTIVATES A DIFFERENT PART OF THE BRAIN THAN PRINTING LETTERS. LEARNING CURSIVE IS ALSO GOOD FOR PRACTICING FINE MOTOR SKILLS.

3. THE PHYSICAL ACT OF WRITING IN CURSIVE LEADS TO A HIGHER LEVEL OF COMPREHENSION. ADDITIONALLY, WRITING IN CURSIVE IS GENERALLY FASTER THAN WRITING IN PRINT, SO AS CHILDREN GET OLDER IT CAN BE MORE EFFICIENT, ESPECIALLY IN TEST TAKING SCENARIOS.

Thanks

CAPITAL LETTER

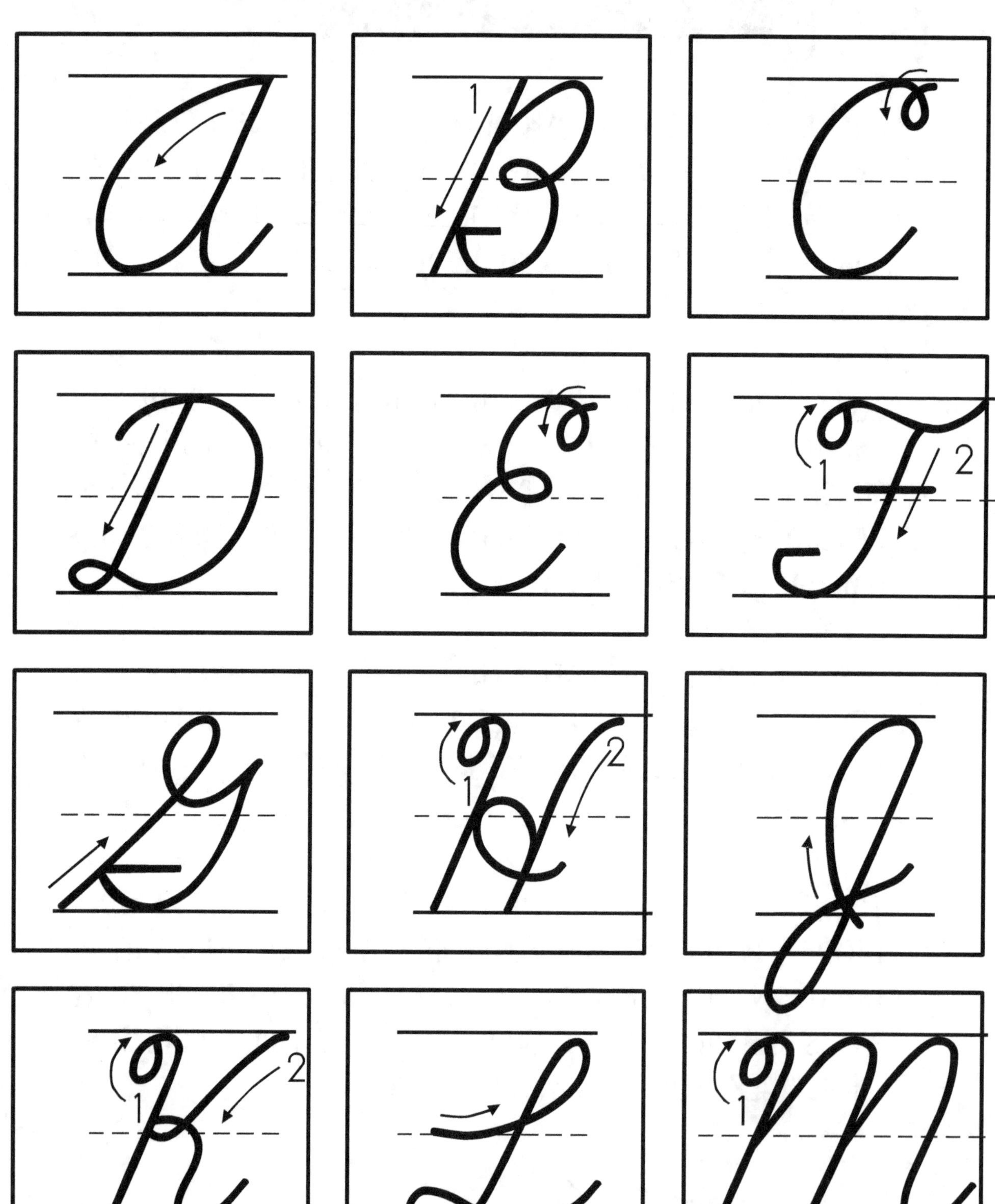

CAPITAL LETTER

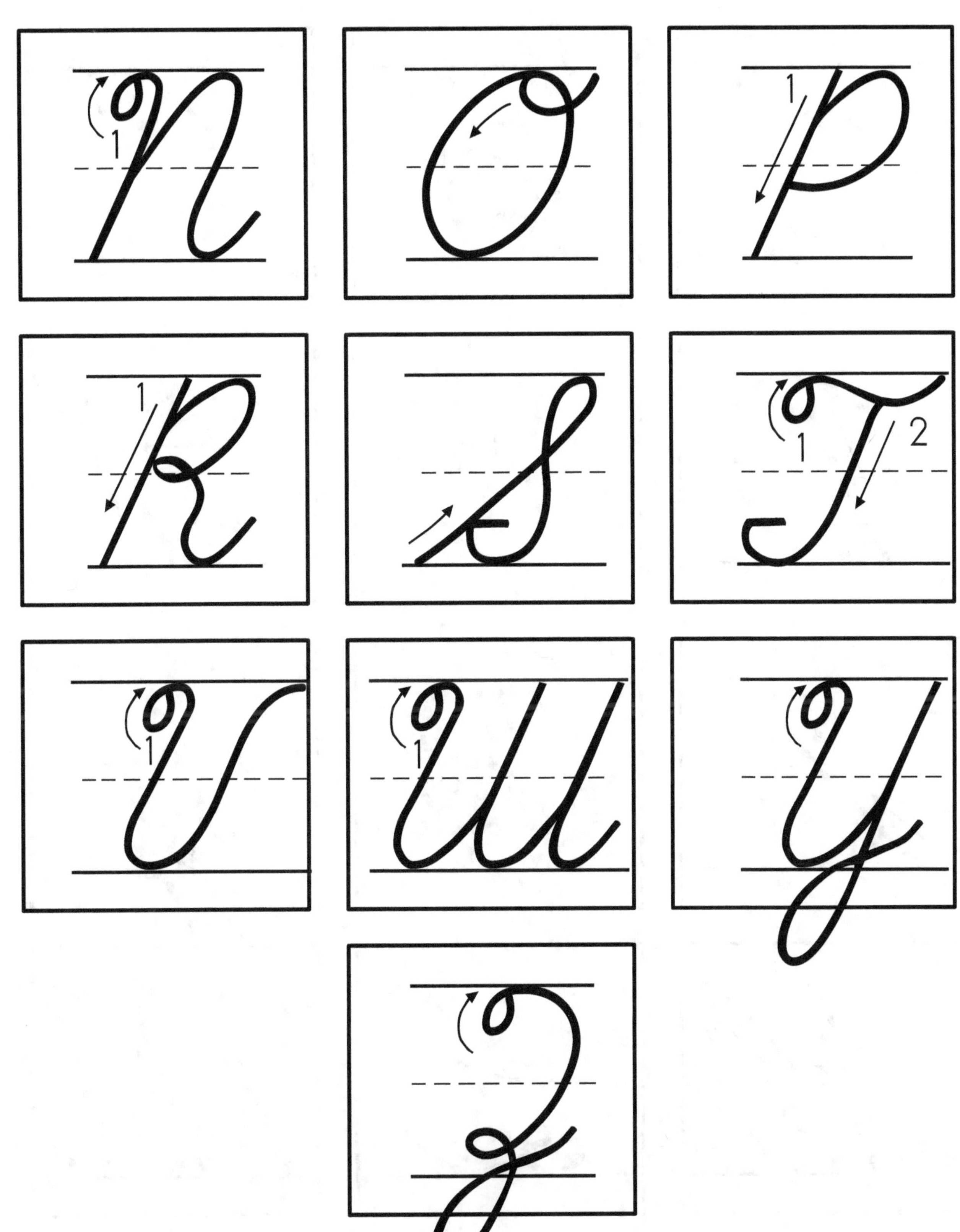

CAPITAL LETTER

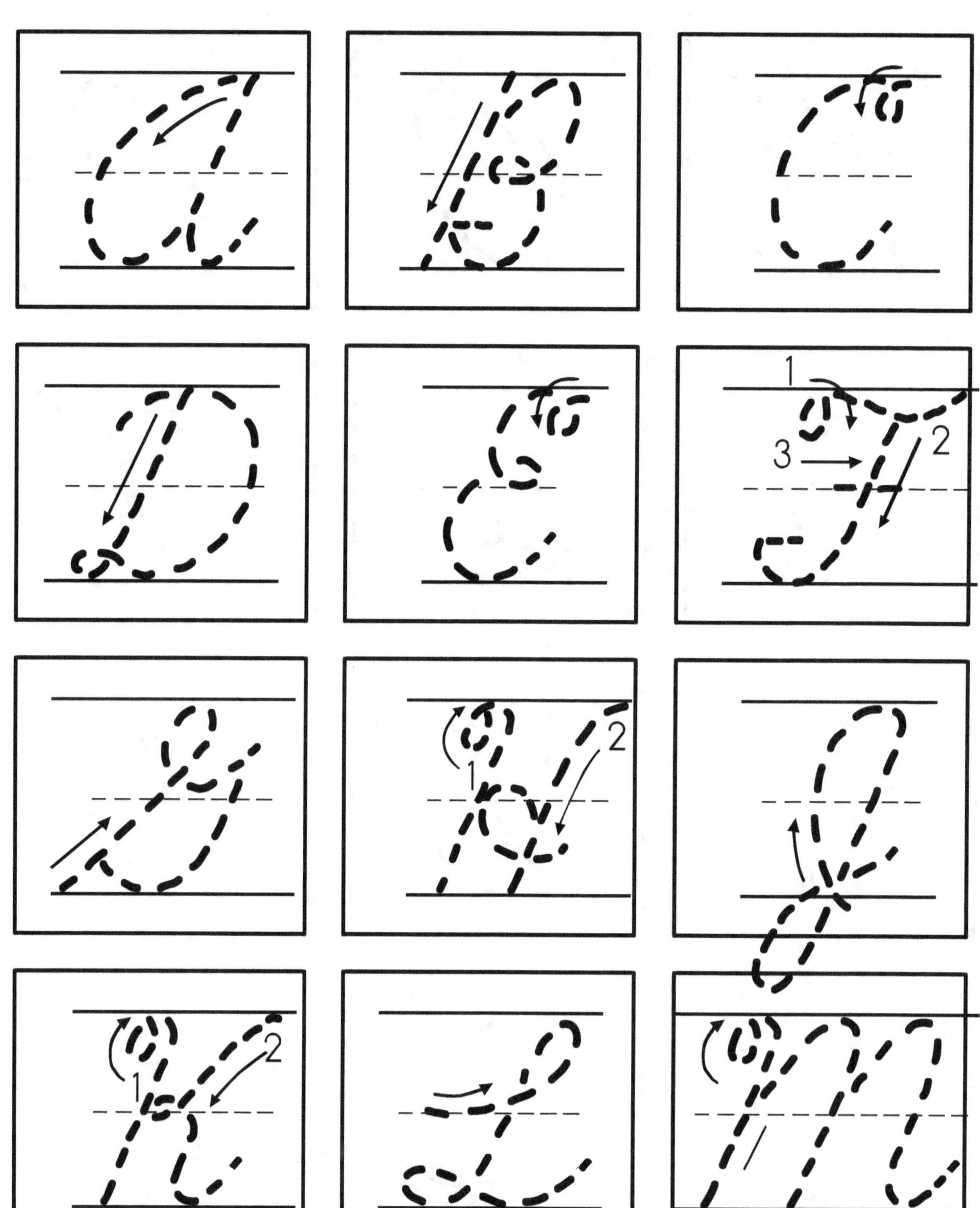

CAPITAL LETTER

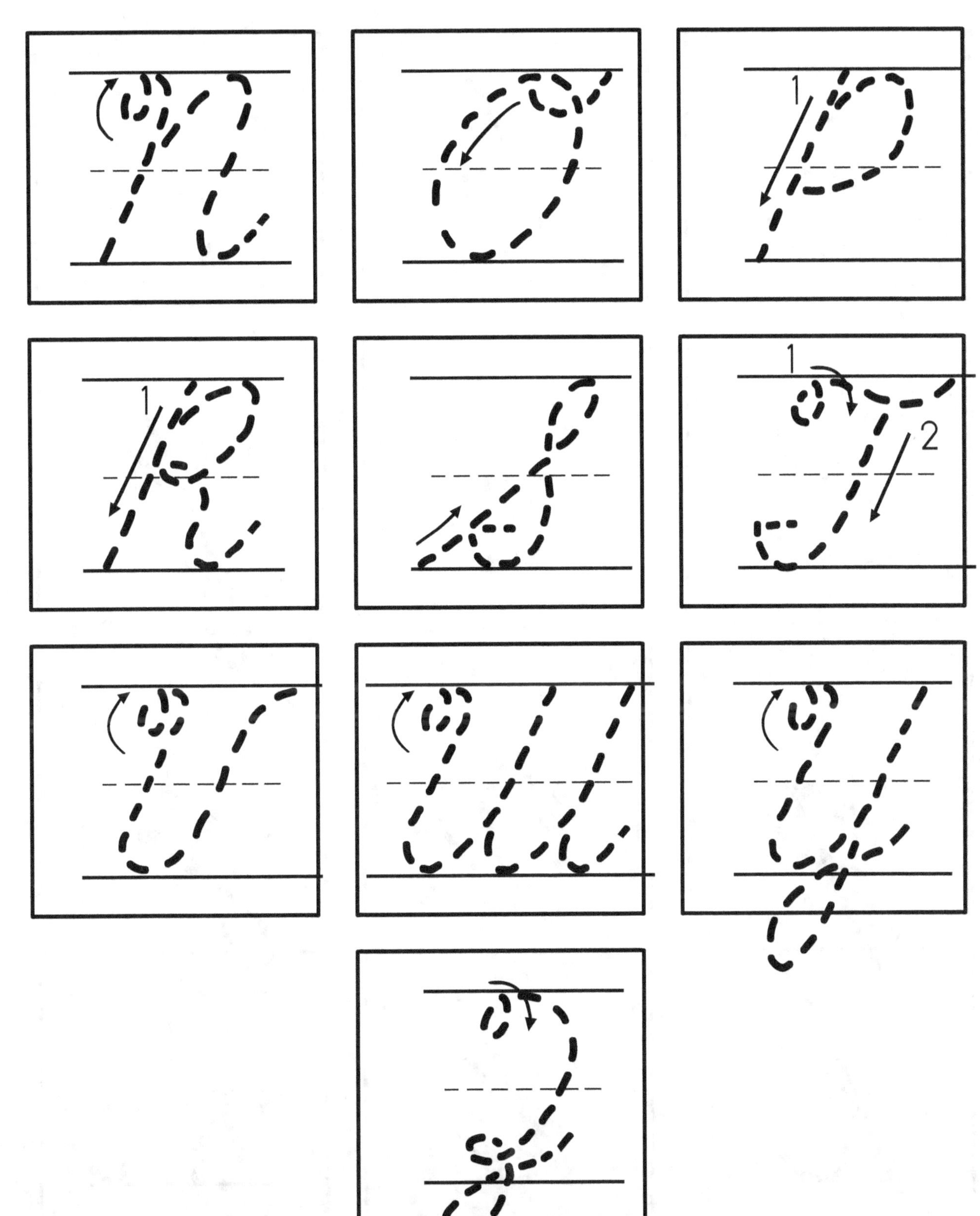

SMALL LETTER

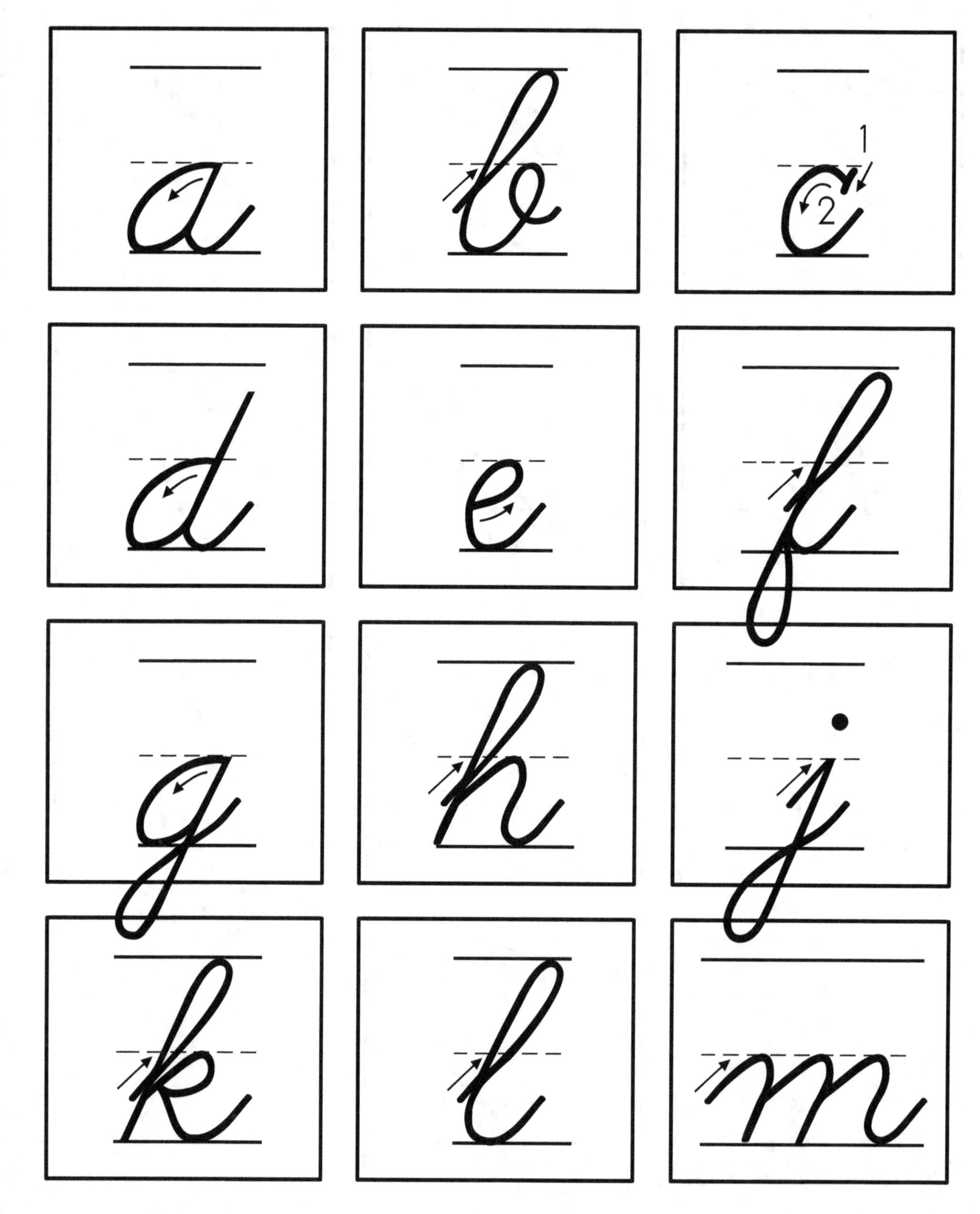

SMALL LETTER

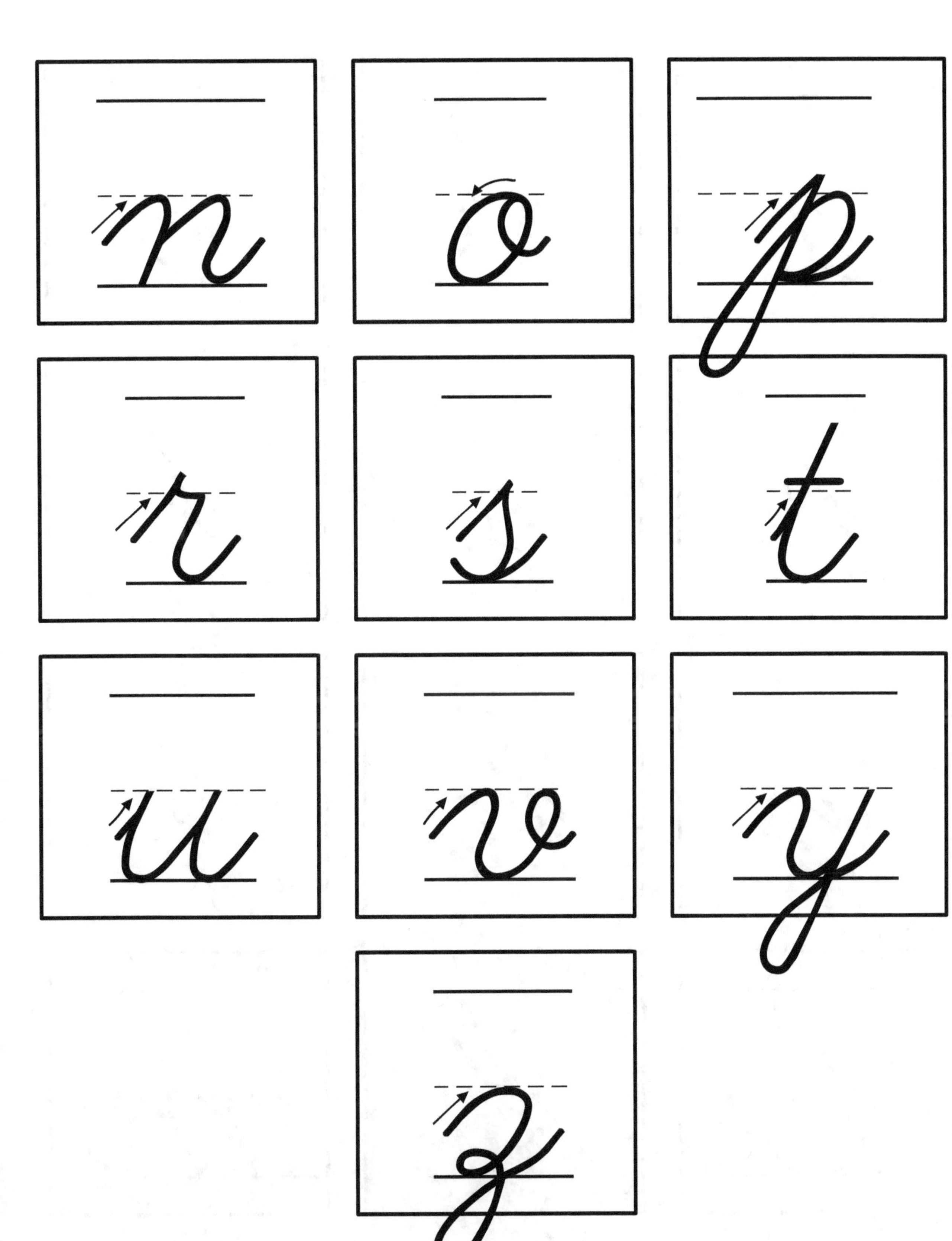

SMALL LETTER

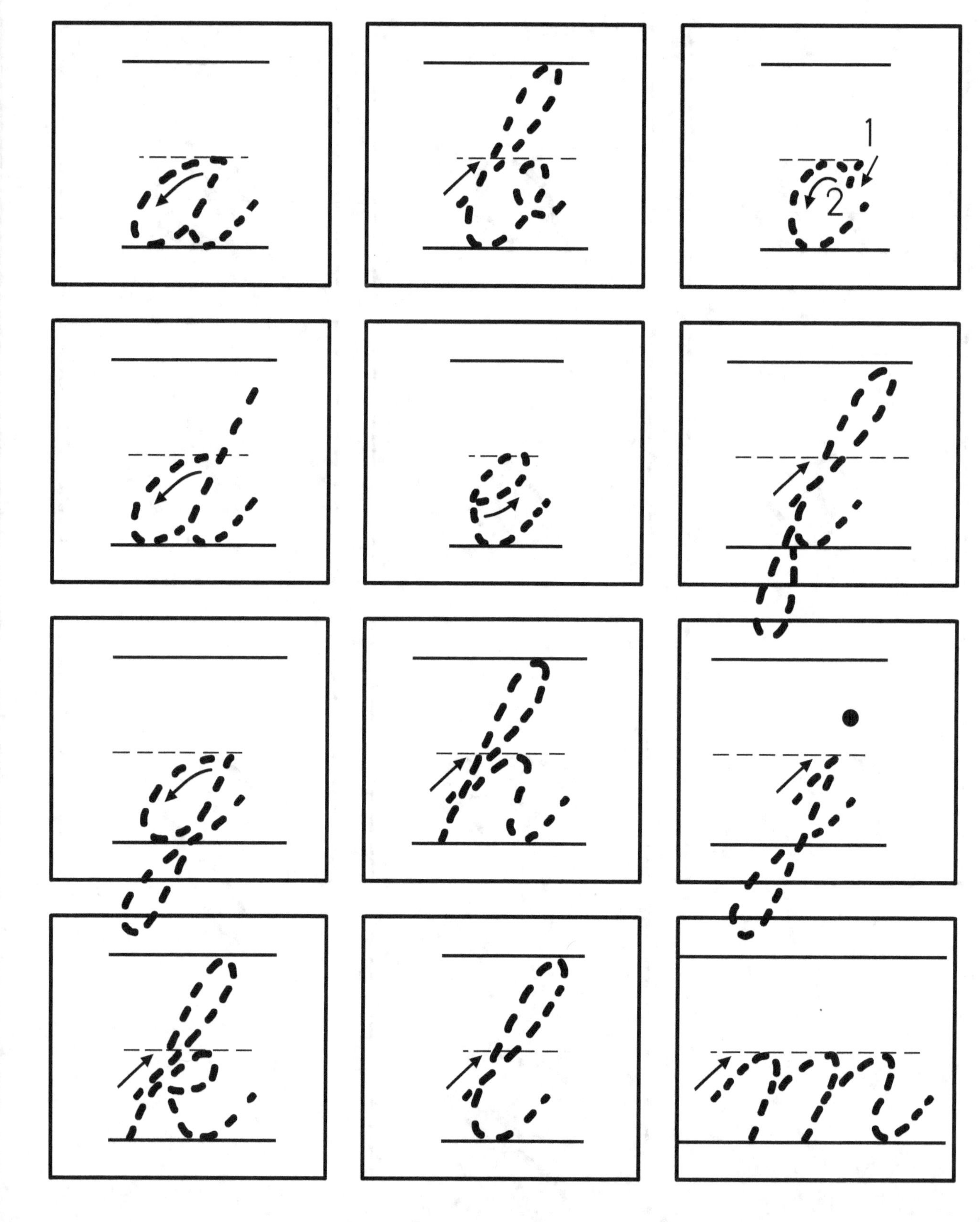

SMALL LETTER

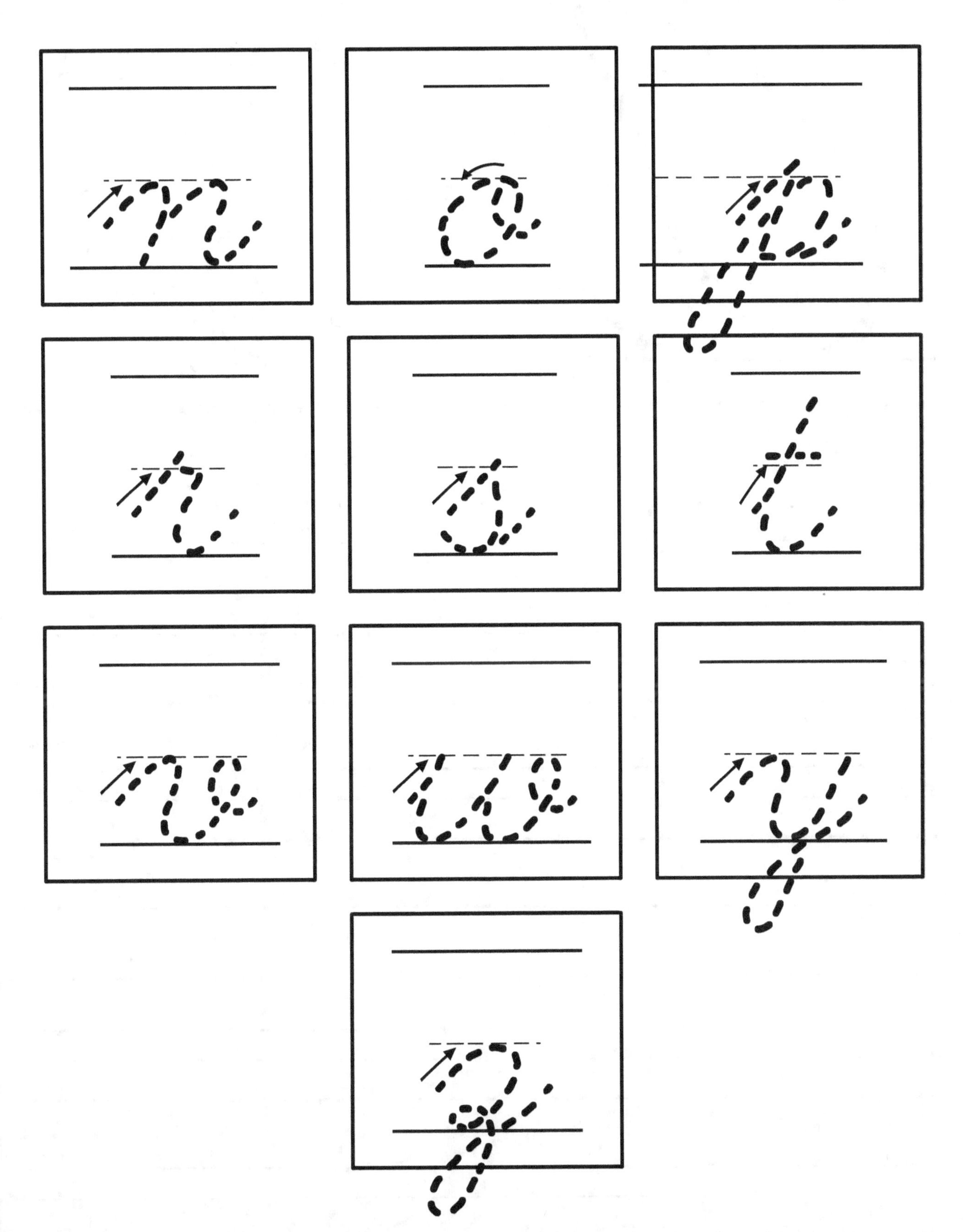

A
Ant   Ant

Ant

Ant

Ant is tiny

Ant is tiny

 COLOR THE ANT

B
Bird

Bird

Bird

Bird can fly

Bird can fly

COLOR THE BIRD

C
C
Cat
Cat

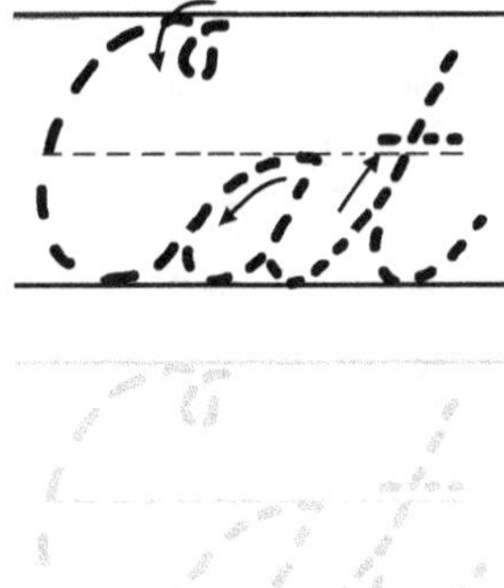

Cat wears hat
Cat wears hat

COLOR THE CAT

D
D
Dog
Dog

TRACE

Dog 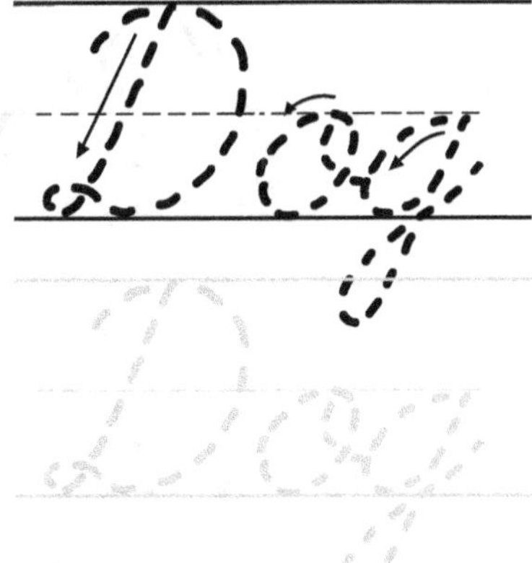

Dog is cute

Dog is cute

COLOR THE DOG

E

Elephant
Elephant

Elephant   Elephant

Elephant   Elephant

Elephant is strong

Elephant is strong

COLOR

COLOR THE ELEPHANT

TRACE

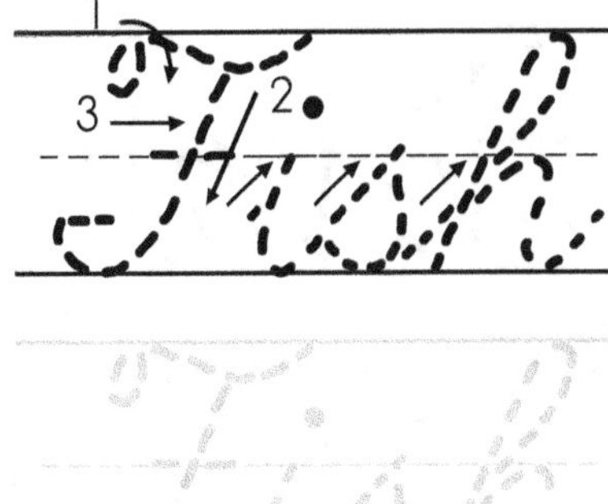
Fish

Fish can swim

Fish can swim

 COLOR THE FISH

Giraffe

Giraffe

Giraffe is tall

COLOR THE GIRAFFE

Hare
Hare

TRACE

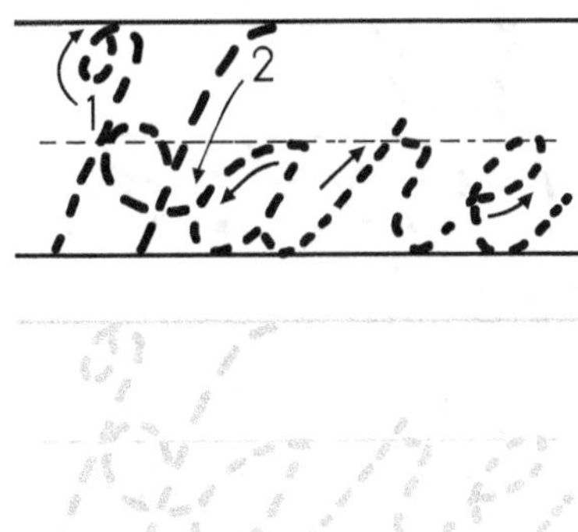

Hare jumps high

Hare jumps high

 COLOR THE HARE

Jj
J
Jaguar
Jaguar

Jaguar

Jaguar

Jaguar has spots

Jaguar has spots

 COLOR THE JAGUAR

Koala
Koala

Koala

Koala

Koala eats bamboo
Koala eats bamboo

COLOR THE KOALA

L
L
Lion
Lion

Lion   Lion

Lion   Lion

Lion is brave

Lion is brave

 COLOR THE LION

M
M
Monkey
Monkey

Monkey Monkey
Monkey Monkey

Monkey eats banana
Monkey eats banana

⚡ COLOR THE MONKEY

N
Newt
Newt

Newt   Newt

Newt eats worms

Newt eats worms

 COLOR THE **NEWT**

Otter
Otter

Otter

Otter

Otter

Otter

Otter is energetic

Otter is energetic

COLOR

COLOR THE OTTER

P
Pig
Pig

Pig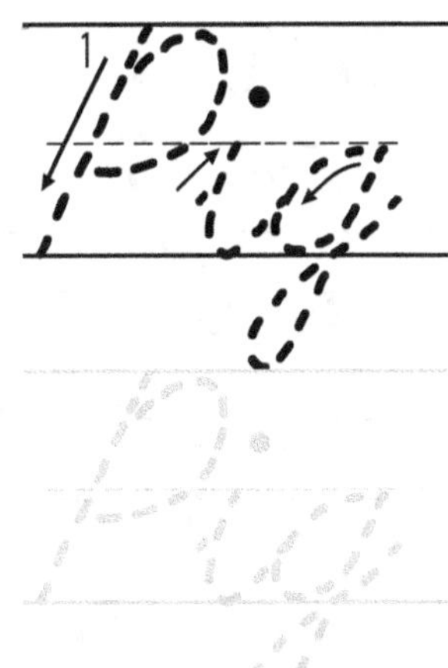

Pig loves mud

Pig loves mud

COLOR THE PIG

R
1
Rhino
Rhino

Rhino Rhino

Rhino Rhino

Rhino has horn

Rhino has horn

⚡ COLOR THE RHINO

S
Seal
Seal

Seal

Seal

Seal eats fish

Seal eats fish

COLOR THE SEAL

1
2
Turtle
Turtle

TRACE

Turtle

Turtle

Turtle

Turtle

Turtle has shell

Turtle has shell

COLOR THE **TURTLE**

V
1
Vole
Vole

Vole

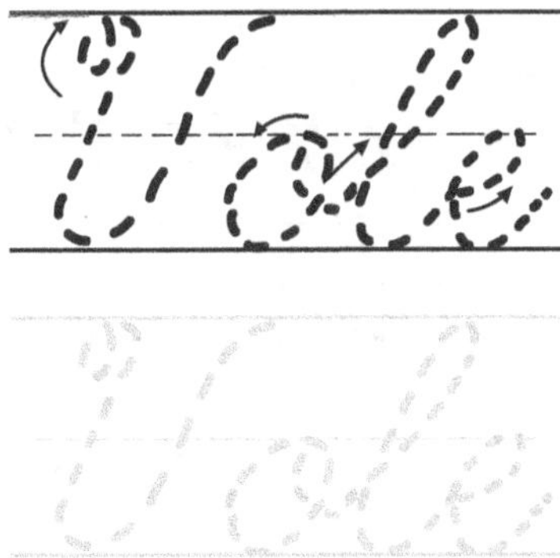

Vole digs hole

COLOR

COLOR THE VOLE

U
Whale
Whale

Whale Whale

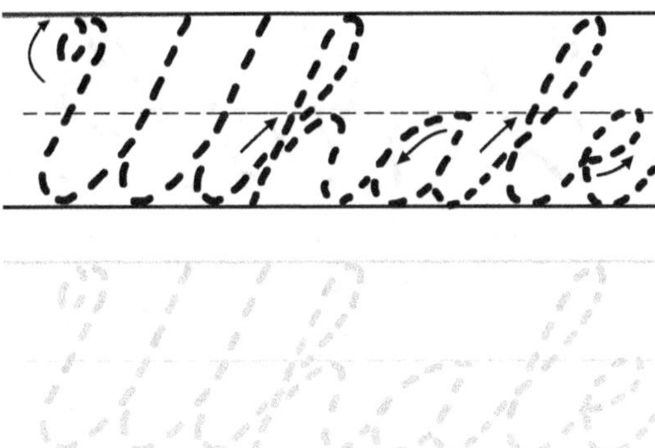

Whale blows air
Whale blows air

COLOR THE WHALE

Y
Y
Yak
Yak

Yak

Yak

Yak

Yak

Yak is friendly

Yak is friendly

 COLOR THE YAK

Zebra
Zebra

Zebra has strips

Zebra has strips

COLOR THE ZEBRA

NOTES

NOTES

NOTES

NOTES

www.ingramcontent.com/pod-product-compliance
Lightning Source LLC
Chambersburg PA
CBHW081915120726
47996CB00010B/3333